Tools of Science

Brigid Rourke

I0880466

Rosen Readers

Rosen Classroom™

New York

Published in 2014 by The Rosen Publishing Group, Inc.
29 East 21st Street, New York, NY 10010

Book Design: Jon D'Rozario

Photo Credits: Cover olivier/Shutterstock.com; pp. 5, 7 (girl) American Images Inc/Digital Vision/Getty Images; p. 7 (aquarium) Dobermaraner/Shutterstock.com; p. 9 (boy) Pressmaster/Shutterstock.com; p. 9 (ladybug) Kletr/Shutterstock.com; p. 11 erashov/Shutterstock.com; p. 13 (digital scale) Vladislav Gajic/Shutterstock.com; p. 13 (balance scale) Huntstock/Thinkstock.com; p. 15 anyaivanova/Shutterstock.com; p. 17 Africa Studio/Shutterstock.com; p. 19 Noam Armonn/Shutterstock.com; p. 21 Matej Kastelic/Shutterstock.com.

ISBN: 978-1-4777-2325-8
6-pack ISBN: 978-1-4777-2326-5

Manufactured in the United States of America

CPSIA Compliance Information: Batch #CS13RC: For further information contact Rosen Publishing, New York, New York at 1-800-237-9932.

Contents

Nadia's Science Class	4
A Closer Look!	8
Tools for Measuring	10
Fun with Funnels!	16
Staying Safe	18
A Future Scientist!	20
What Does It Measure?	22
Glossary	23
Index	24

Nadia's Science Class

Nadia's **favorite** class in school is science class. She loves to learn about nature. During science class, Nadia learns about plants, animals, rocks, and even weather! Nadia and her classmates use different science tools to help them learn.

Mrs. Jackson is Nadia's teacher. She shows students what each tool does and helps them use the tools safely.

Science class is fun! Nadia learns a lot from Mrs. Jackson.

400 mL
PYREX®

Nadia uses a journal every day in science class. She uses it to report on the things she sees and does in class. Mrs. Jackson asks her students to write about the world around them in their journals.

Nadia's classroom has an aquarium in it. Many little fish live inside it. Sometimes Nadia writes in her journal about the different fish in the aquarium.

Nadia rereads her journal to recall different things she saw and did during science class.

A Closer Look!

Sometimes Mrs. Jackson asks Nadia and her classmates to draw pictures of plants and plant parts in their journals. She gives them a magnifying glass to help them see things more clearly. This tool makes things look bigger than they really are. When Nadia looks at a leaf through a magnifying glass, it looks supersized! Nadia's class uses magnifying glasses to look at bugs, too.

Some things look very unusual when you see them through a magnifying glass!

Tools for Measuring

Many of the tools in Nadia's science class are used for measuring. When Nadia needs to measure how long or short something is, she's trying to find its length. One tool for measuring length is a ruler. This tool has **units** called inches and centimeters on it. Mrs. Jackson lines a pencil up with a ruler to show her class how long the pencil is.

Nadia makes sure to recheck the number of units before she writes the pencil's length in her journal.

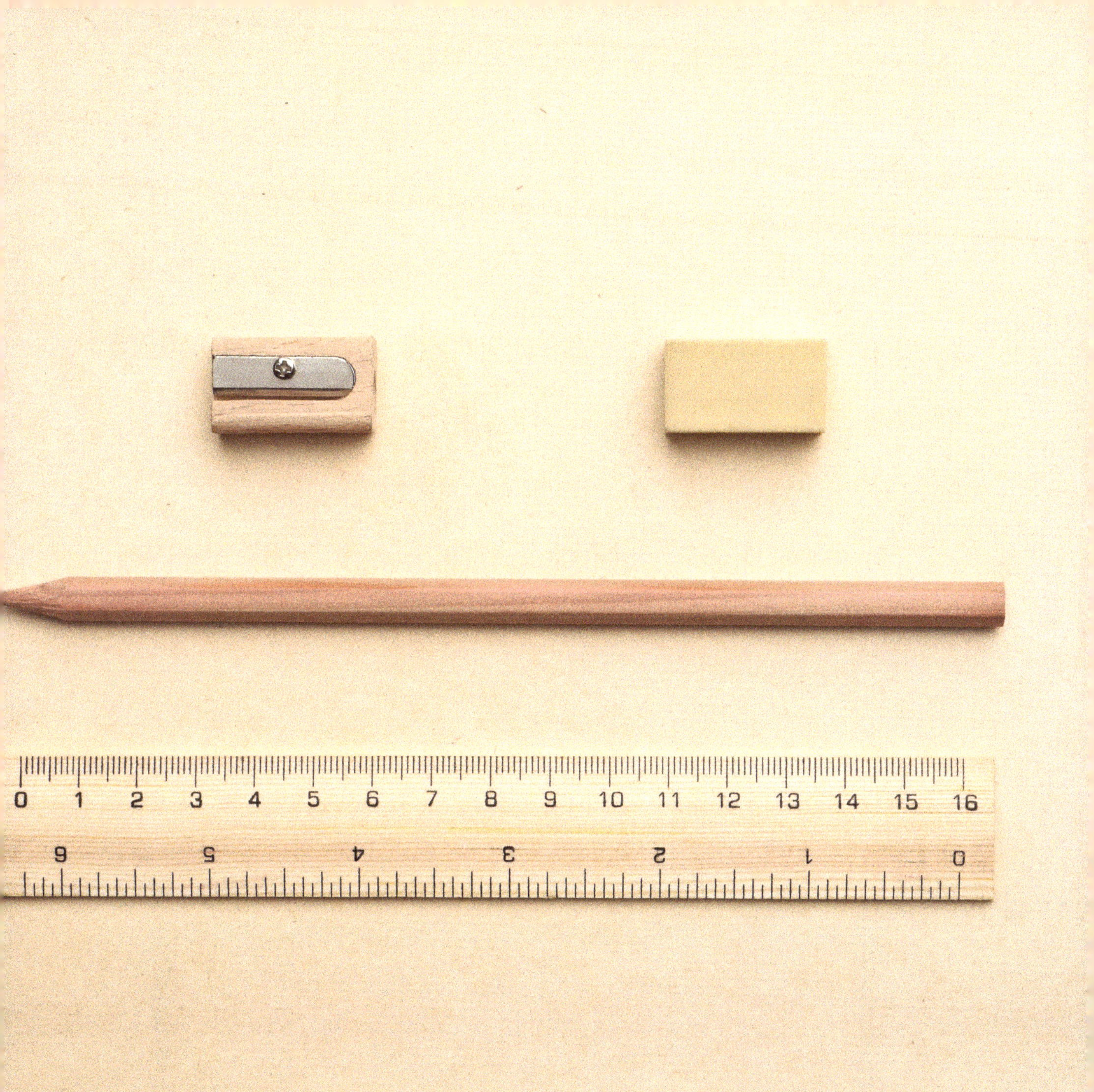
0 1 2 3 4 5 6 7 8 9 10 11 12 13 14 15 16
6 5 4 3 2 1 0

Nadia uses a scale to measure how much something weighs. One kind of scale is a balance scale. It **compares** the weights of two objects. The heavier object makes its side go down, and the lighter object goes up.

Another kind of scale is a digital scale. Mrs. Jackson puts an object on the scale. Then, its weight is shown on a small screen.

The students carefully review the number on the digital scale so they don't make mistakes when they record weights in their journals.

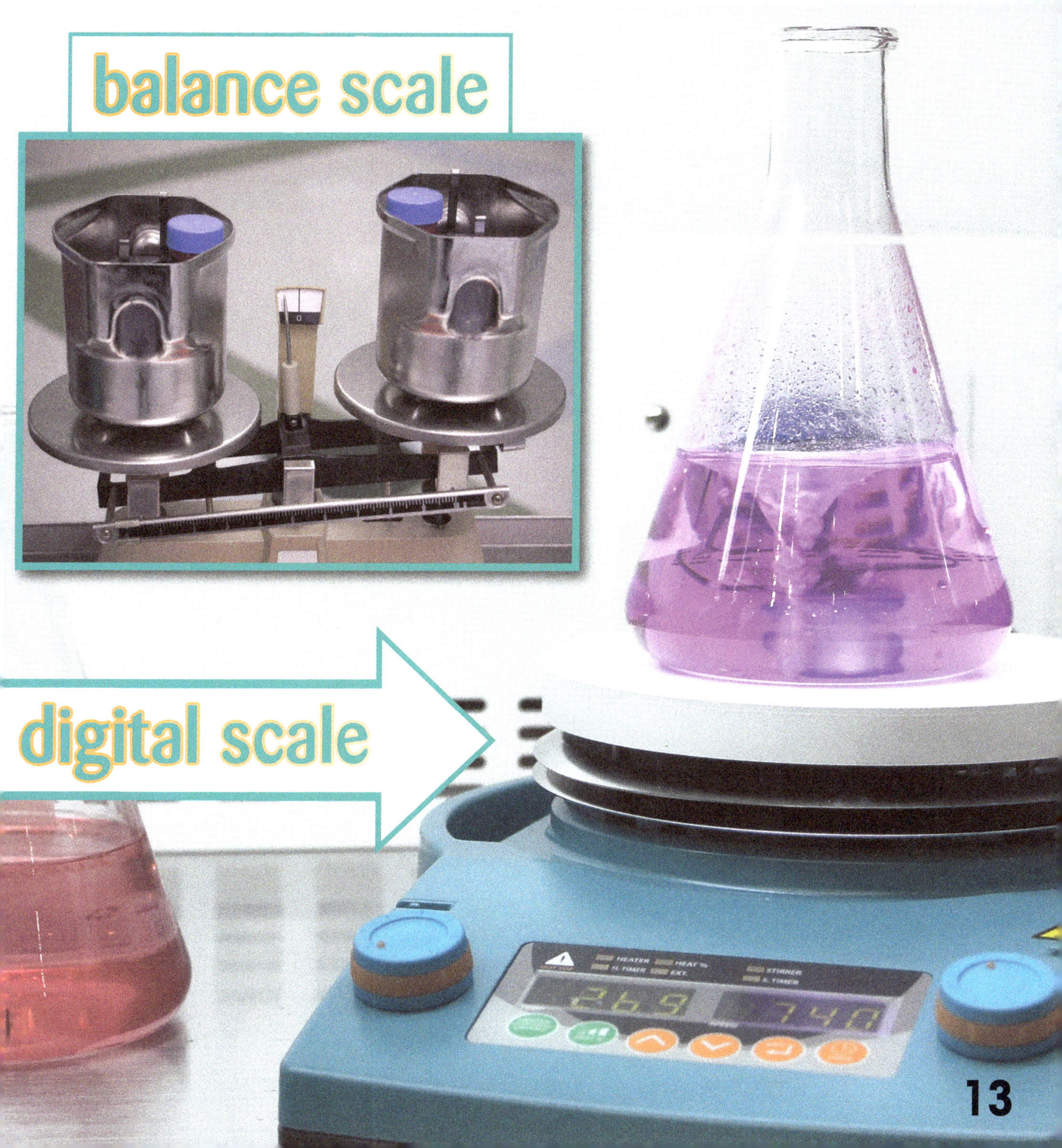
balance scale
digital scale

When Nadia measures how hot or cold something is, she measures its temperature. A thermometer measures temperature. Mrs. Jackson says that a thermometer is a tube full of **liquid**. When the liquid gets warm, it rises. When it gets cool, it drops lower in the tube. Sometimes Nadia uses a digital thermometer, too. It shows the temperature on a small screen.

Temperature is measured in units called degrees. The numbers on the side of the thermometer show the number of degrees.

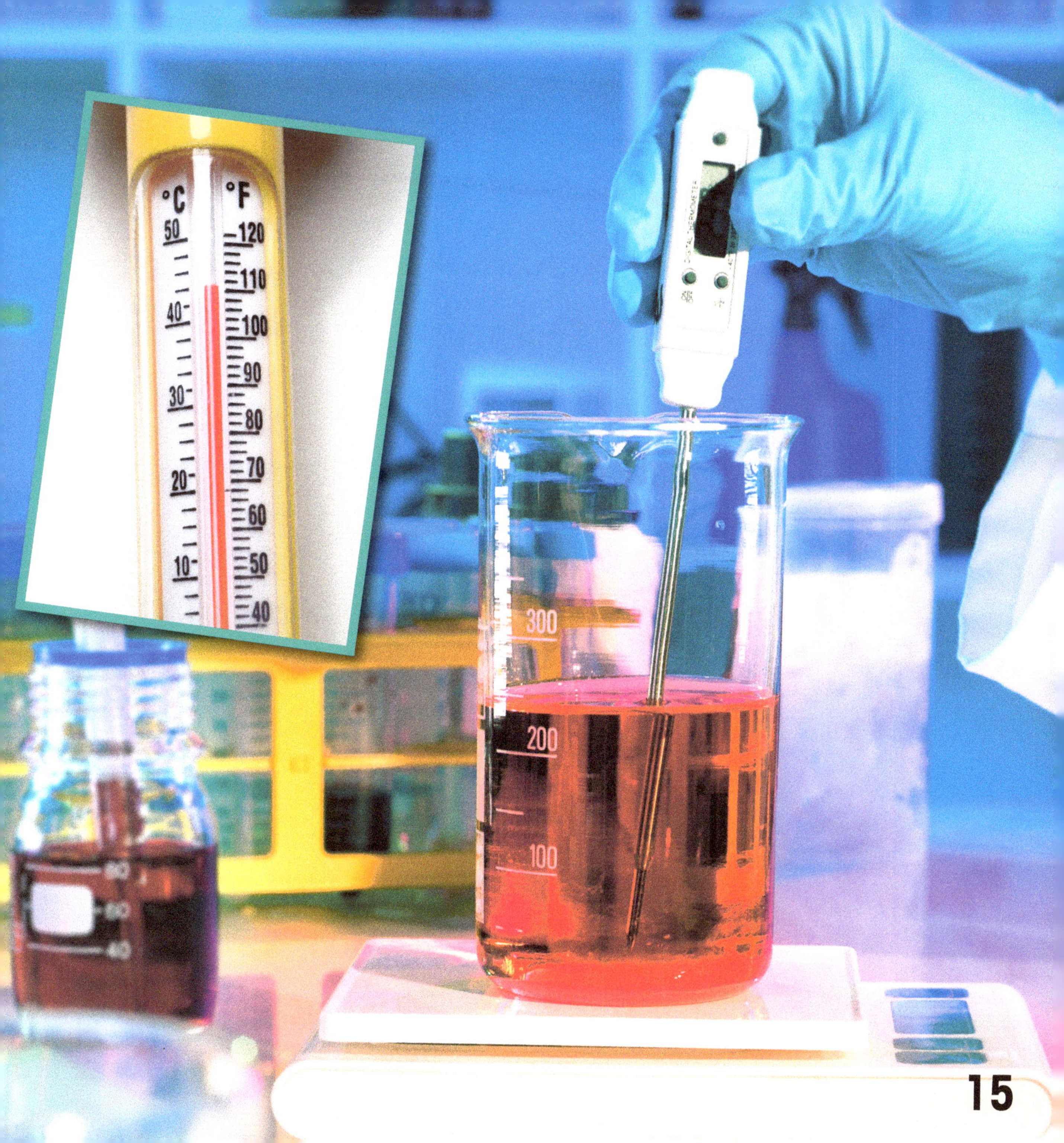
°C
°F
50
40
30
20
10
120
110
100
90
80
70
60
50
40
300
200
100

Fun with Funnels!

There are lots of tools used in science class to hold and **transport** liquids. A beaker looks like a glass jar and is used to measure liquids. Sometimes, Mrs. Jackson puts the liquid from the beaker into smaller **containers**, called test tubes. To do that, she pours the liquid through a funnel, which is wide at the top and narrow at the bottom.

Beakers measure the volume of a liquid. Volume is how much space a liquid takes up.

test tube
funnel
beaker

Staying Safe

You can't overlook safety when you work with science tools! Mrs. Jackson shows her class special safety gloves. These gloves aren't reused after they're worn. They're thrown away, and clean ones are used the next time.

Nadia and her classmates also use special aprons to keep their clothes clean. Some older students even wear special coats in their science classes!

Goggles are another safety tool. They're special glasses that keep your eyes safe.

A Future Scientist!

Learning about science tools makes science class even more fun! Nadia loves that there are always new things to learn and new ways to study the world around her. Using the special tools Mrs. Jackson showed her class makes Nadia feel like a real **scientist**! That's what she wants to be when she grows up.

Some of Nadia's friends are unsure about what they want to be when they grow up. Nadia knows she wants to be a scientist and use science tools every day!

What Does It Measure?

Tool	Measurement	Unit
beaker	volume	cups (liters)
ruler	length	inches (centimeters)
scale	weight	pounds (grams)
thermometer	temperature	degrees

Glossary

compare (kuhm-PEHR) To study two or more things in order to find what is the same and different about them.

container (kuhn-TAY-nuhr) An object used to hold something.

favorite (FAY-vuh-ruht) Liked best.

liquid (LIH-kwuhd) Something that flows freely like water.

scientist (SY-uhn-tihst) Someone who studies the way things work and the way things are.

transport (TRANS-port) To move something from one place to another.

unit (YOO-nuht) A standard used for measuring.

Index

aprons, 18
beaker, 16, 22
centimeters, 10, 22
coats, 18
degrees, 14, 22
funnel, 16
goggles, 18
inches, 10, 22
journal(s), 6, 8, 10, 12
length, 10, 22
liquid(s), 14, 16
magnifying glass(es), 8
ruler, 10, 22
safety, 18
safety gloves, 18
scale, 12, 22
temperature, 14, 22
test tubes, 16
thermometer, 14, 22
volume, 16, 22
weight(s), 12, 22